BONUS!

Pick up your FREE BONUS sweary word coloring pages!

Check out: **www.FckYeahColoring.com**

For more BONUS pages like this...

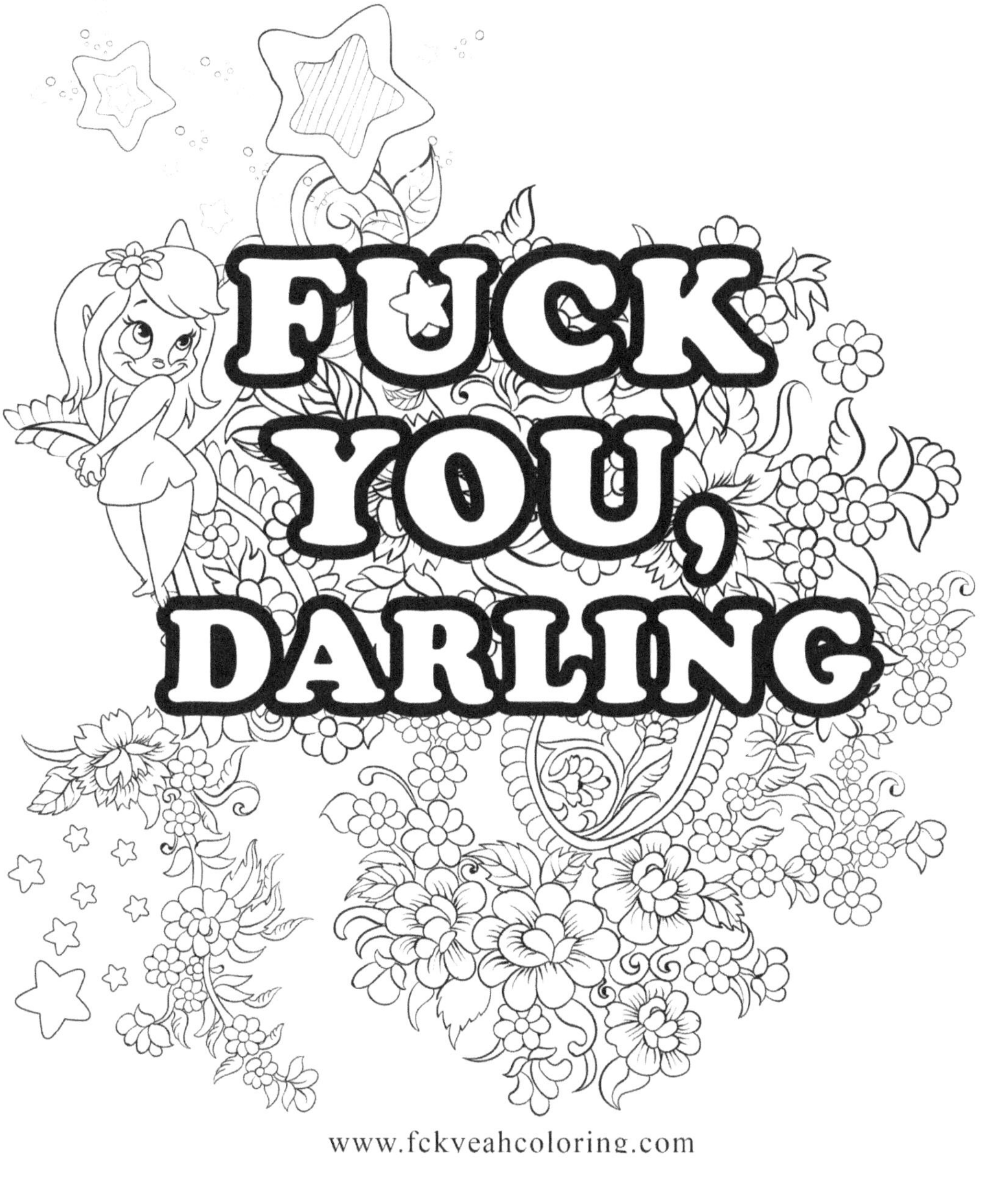

Dear Creative,

Have a giggle and blow off some steam!

Look through the pages, and pick out the swears that speak to you at the moment.

Just remember, these pages are 18+ and not for the faint-hearted!

I send out NEW, FREE bonus pages every couple of weeks

as a special thank you.

Grab your ridiculously crude new pages at **www.FckYeahColoring.com**

Make sure you get printable BONUS sweary coloring pages

delivered immediately!

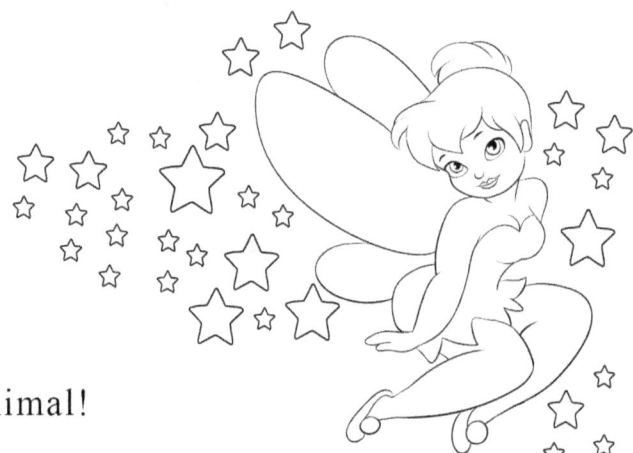

Now, enjoy coloring, you filthy animal!

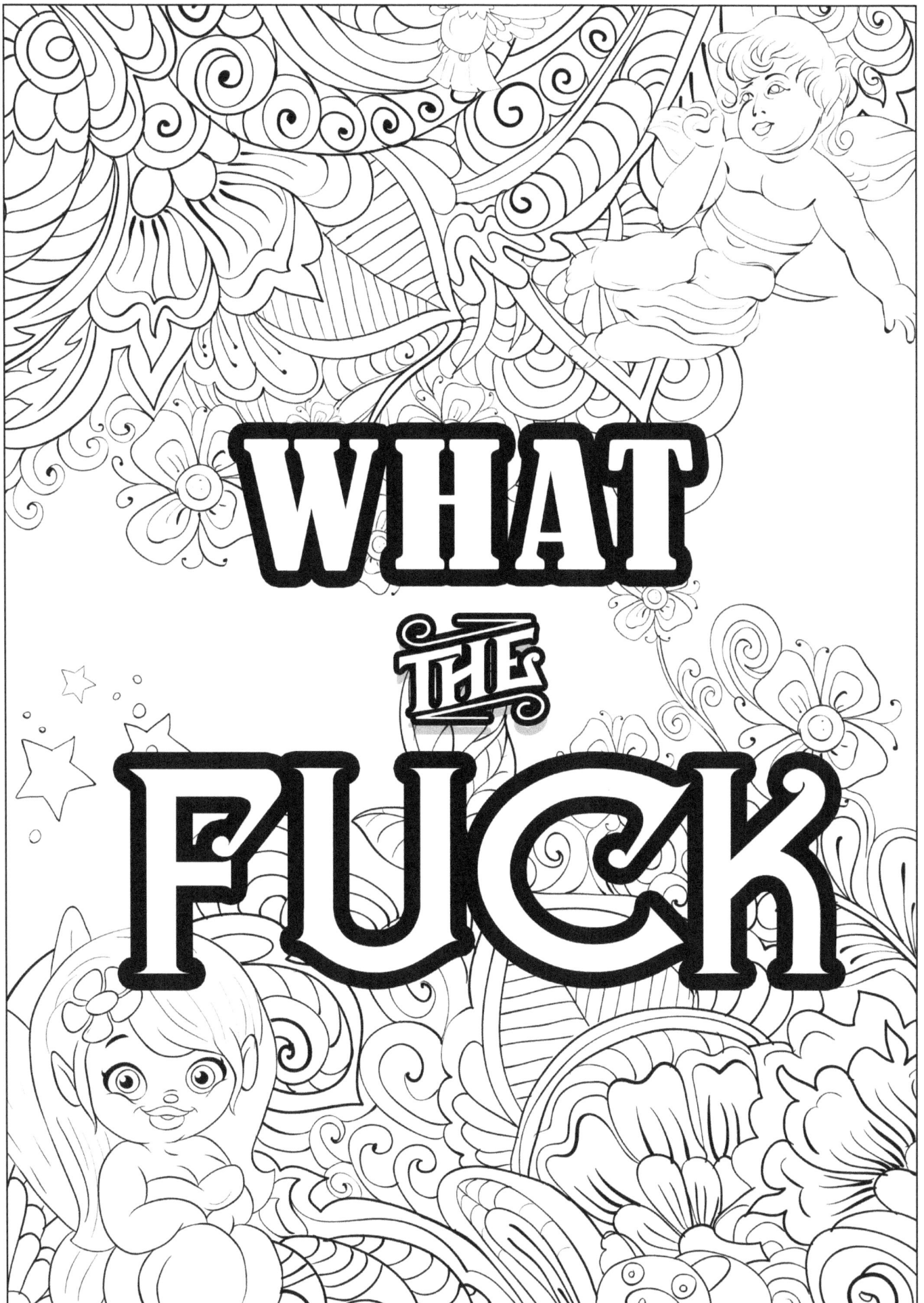

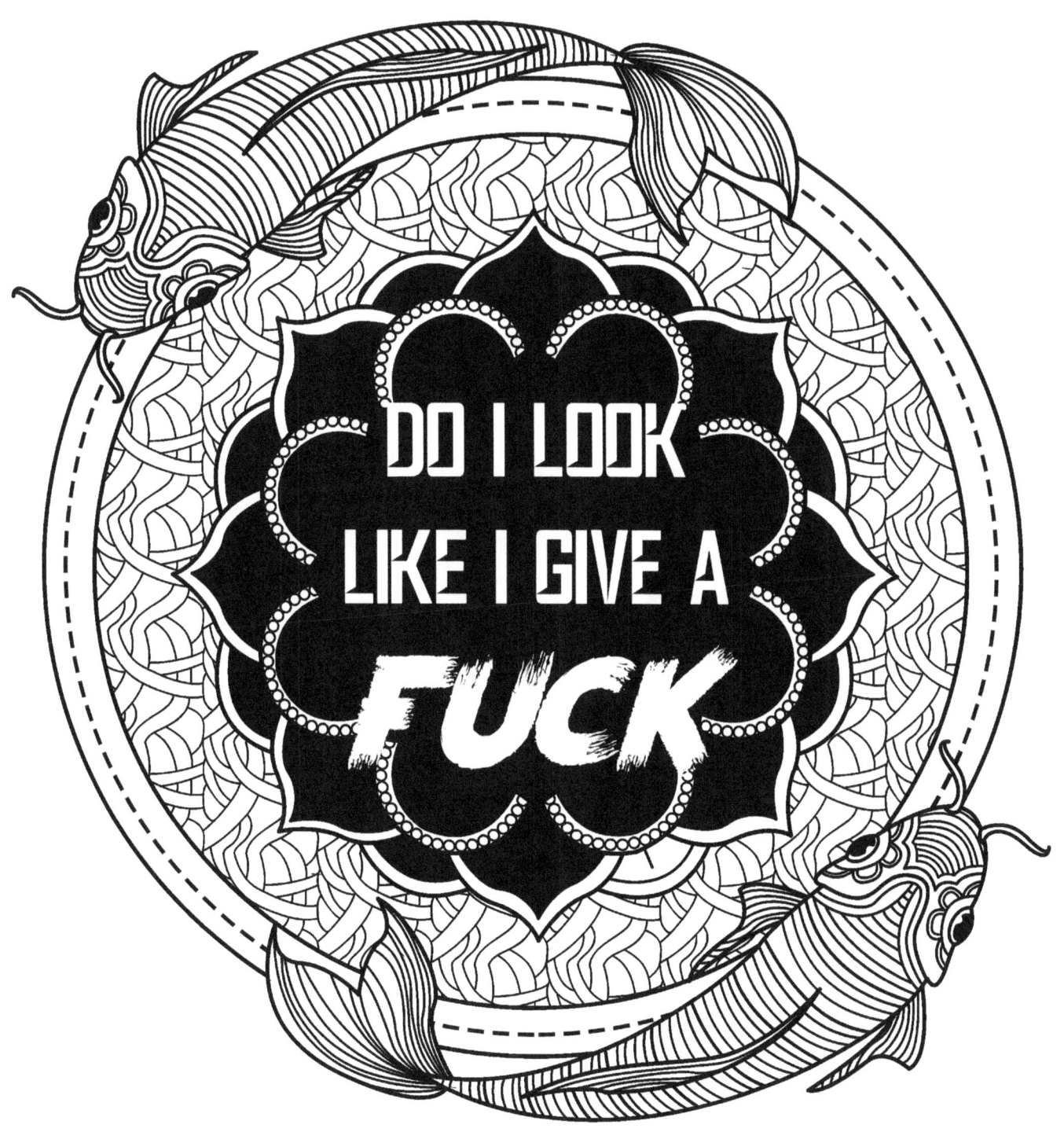

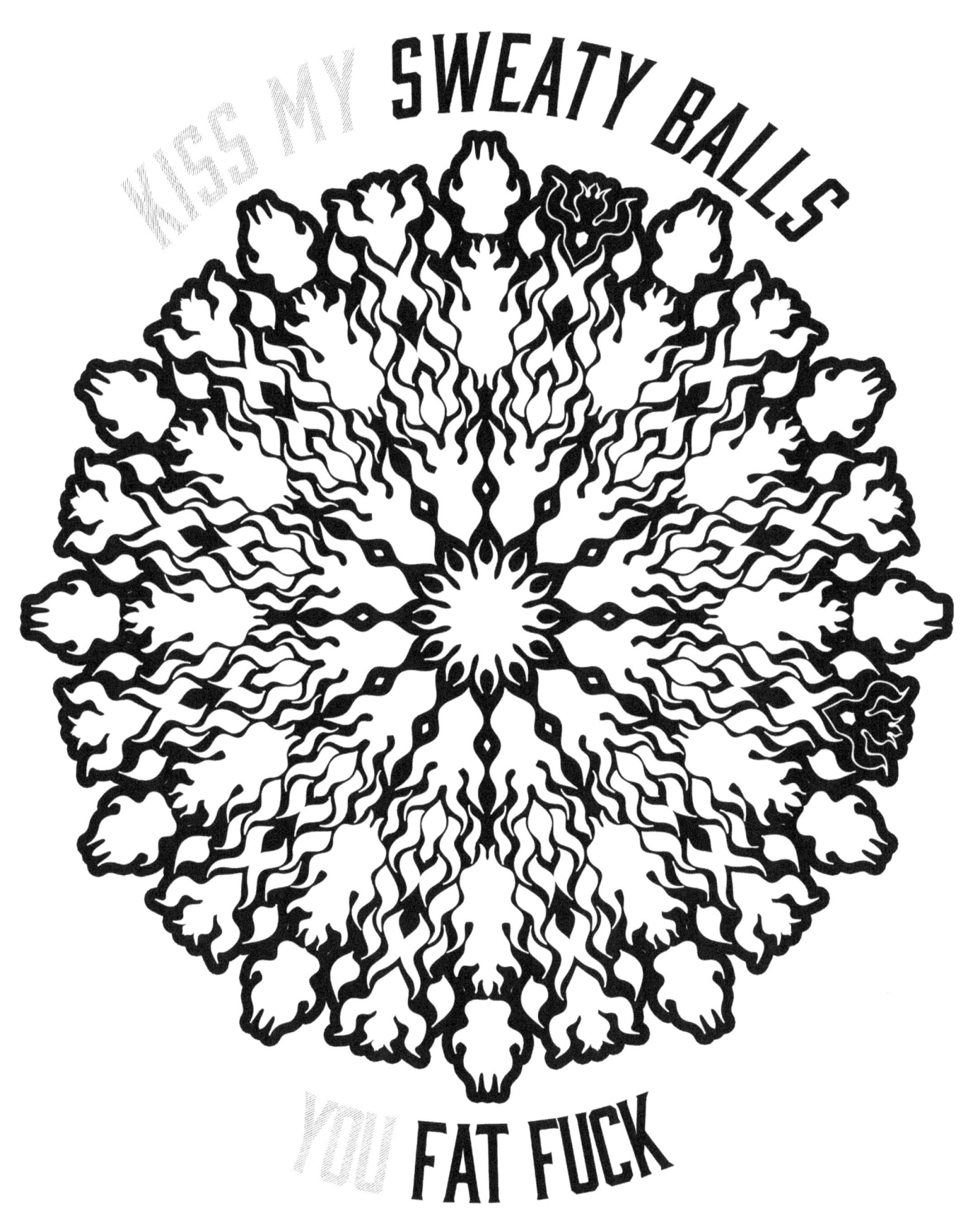

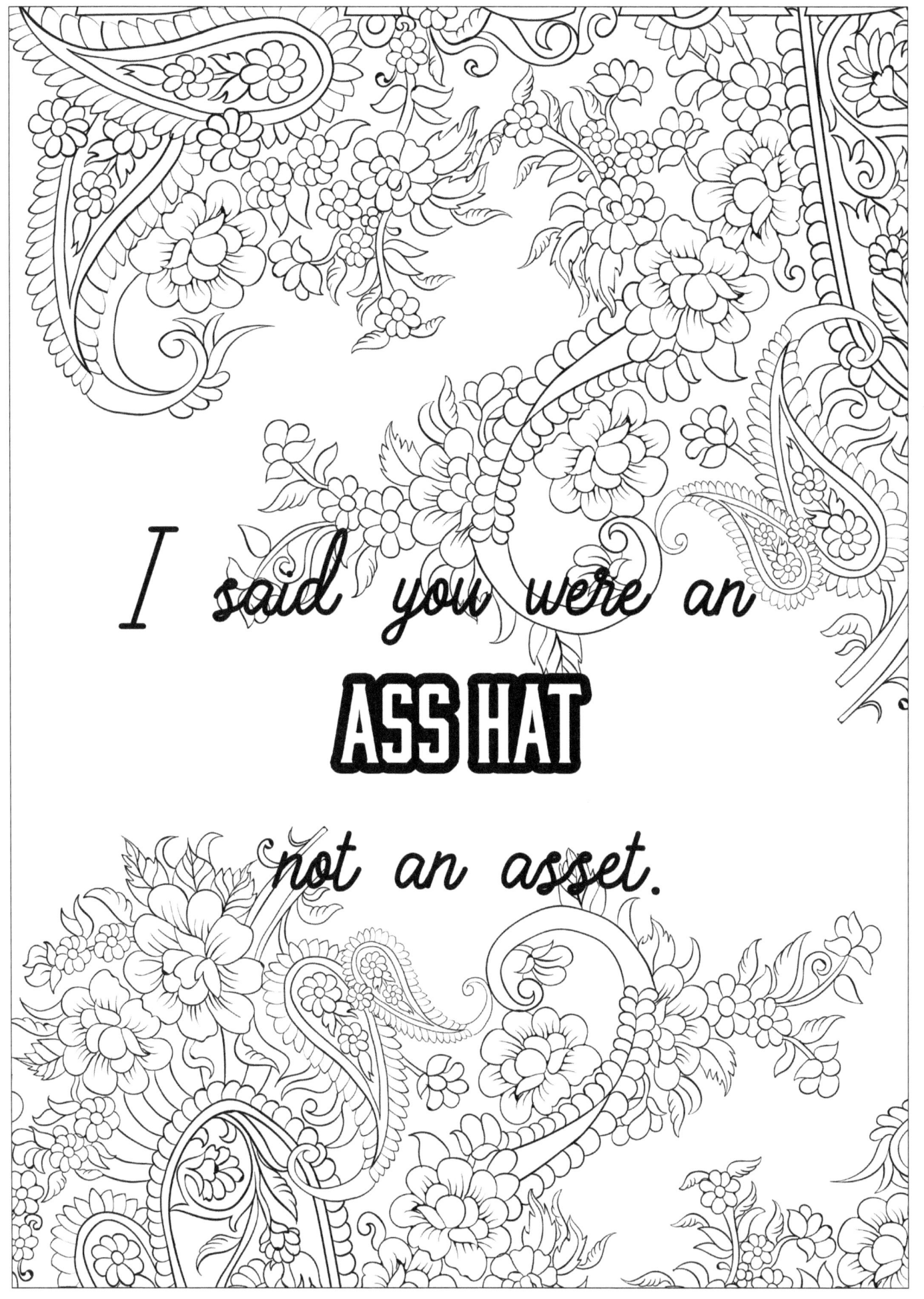

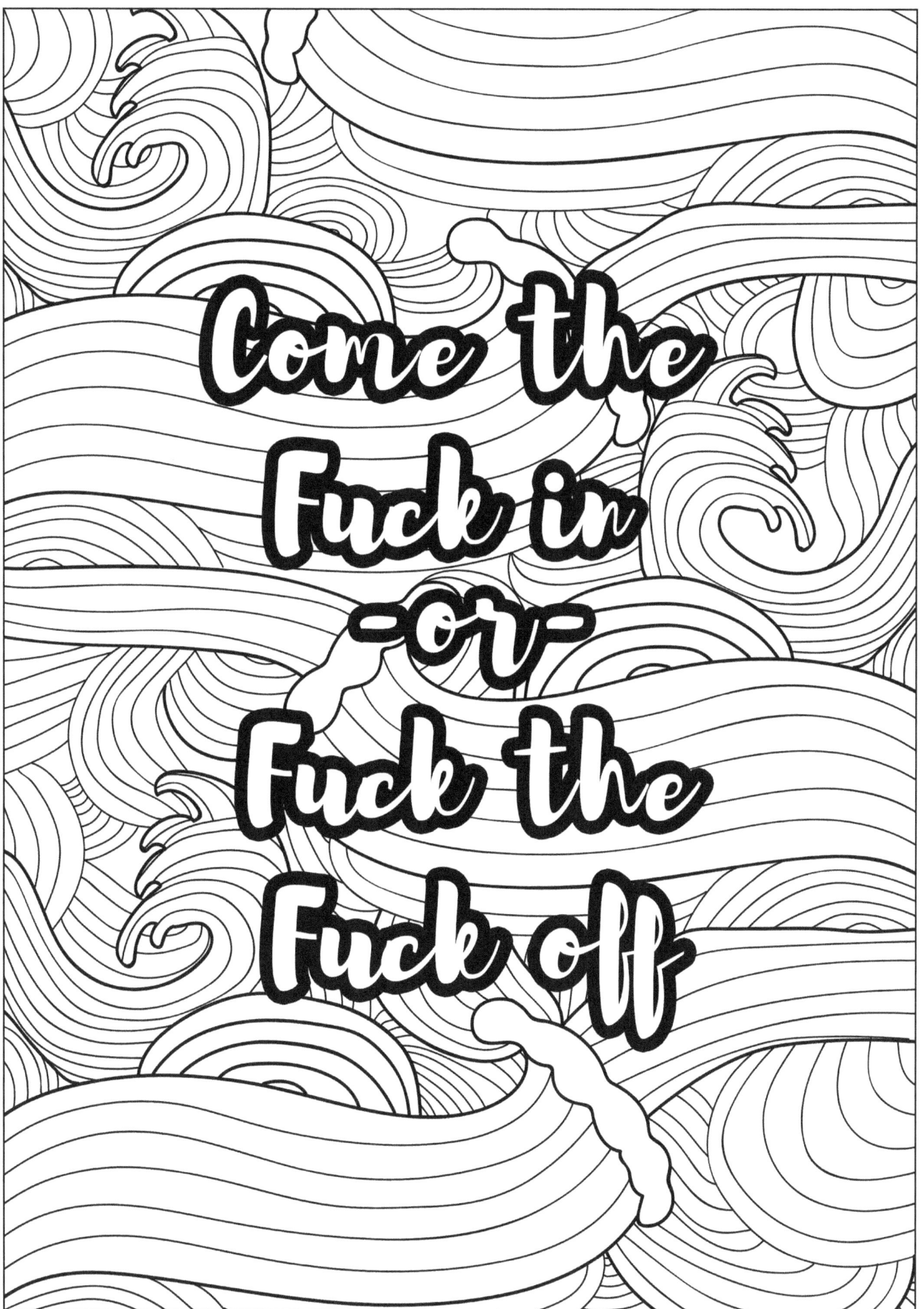

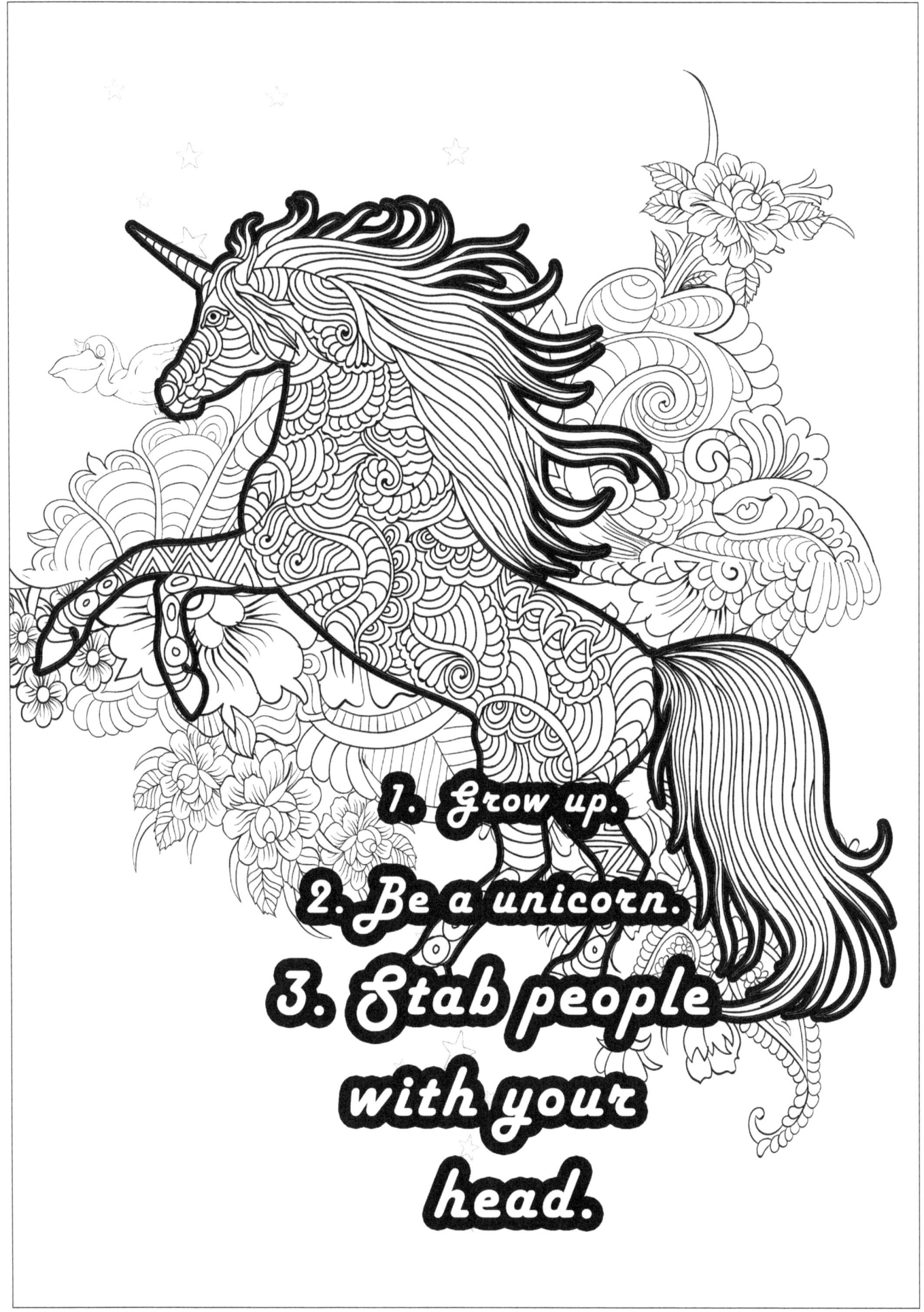

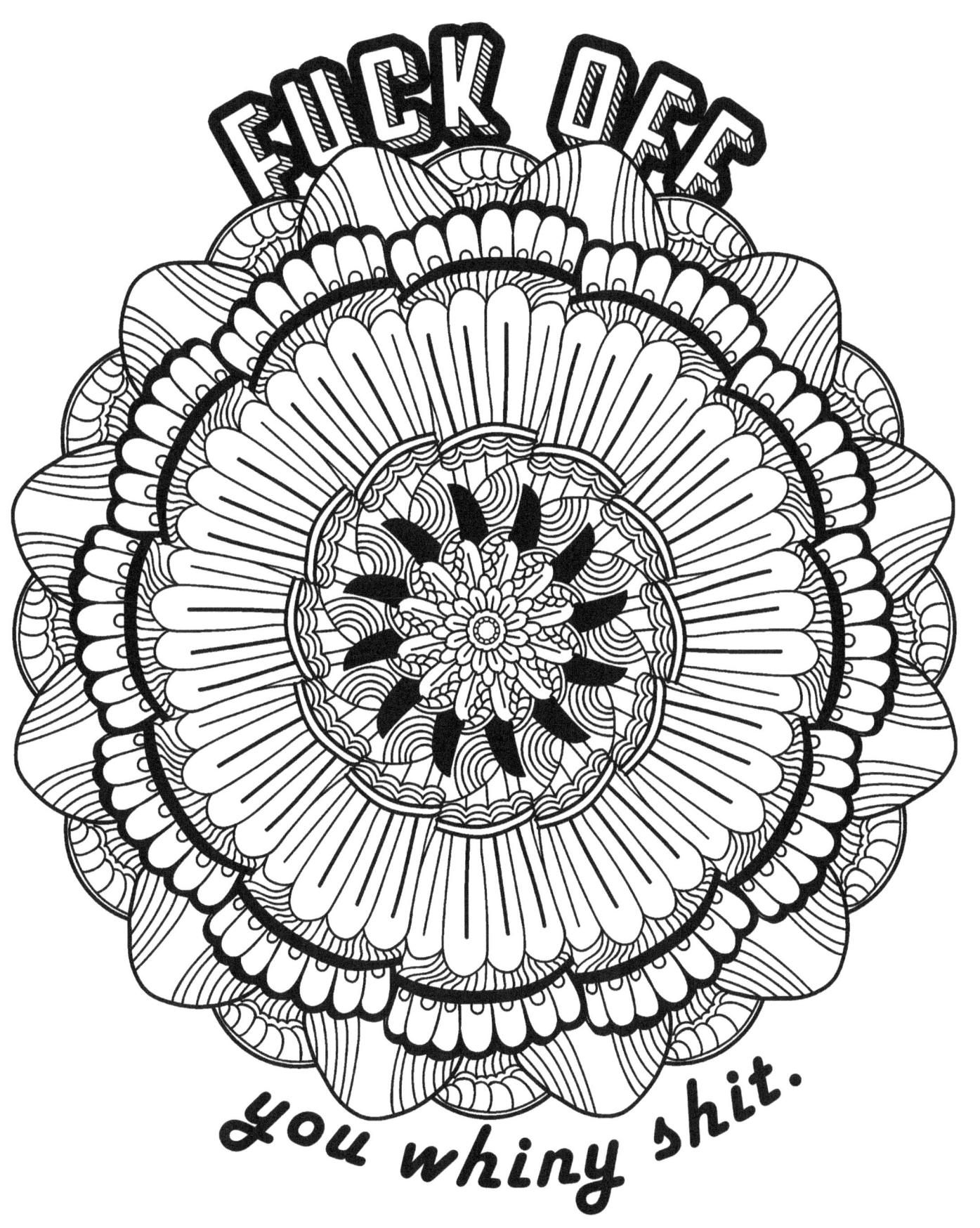

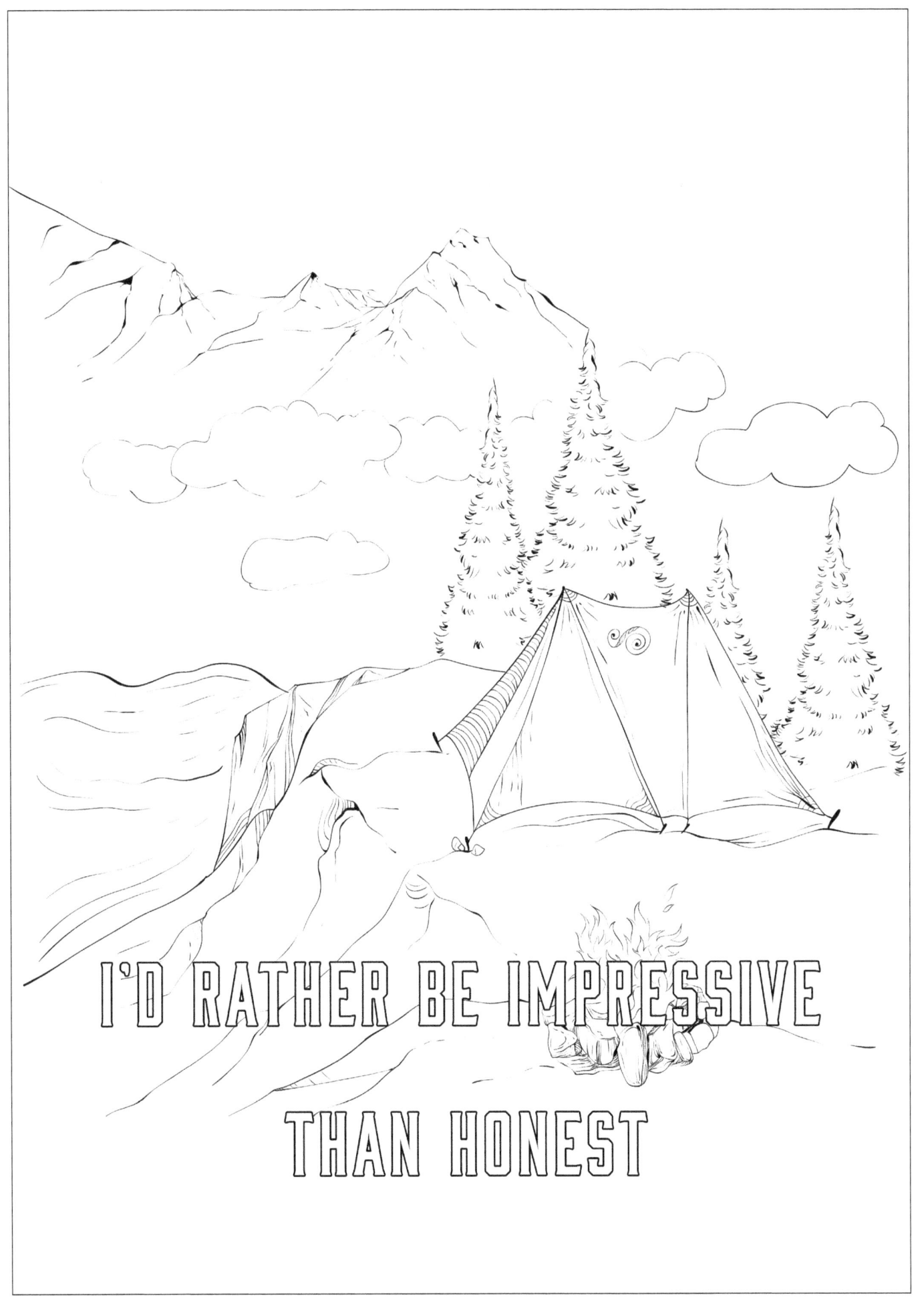

PEOPLE CHANGE.
NOW I'M A DRAGON

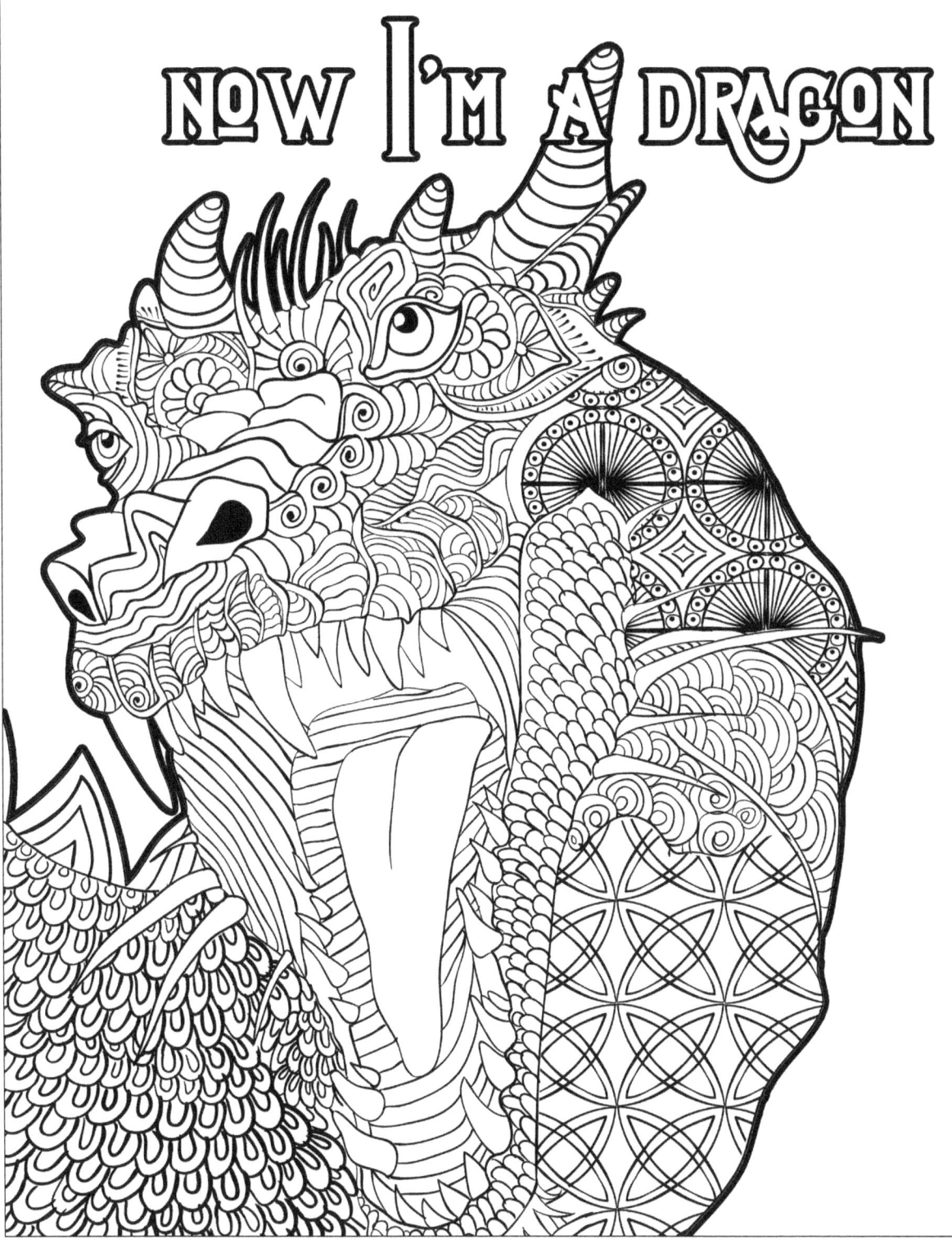

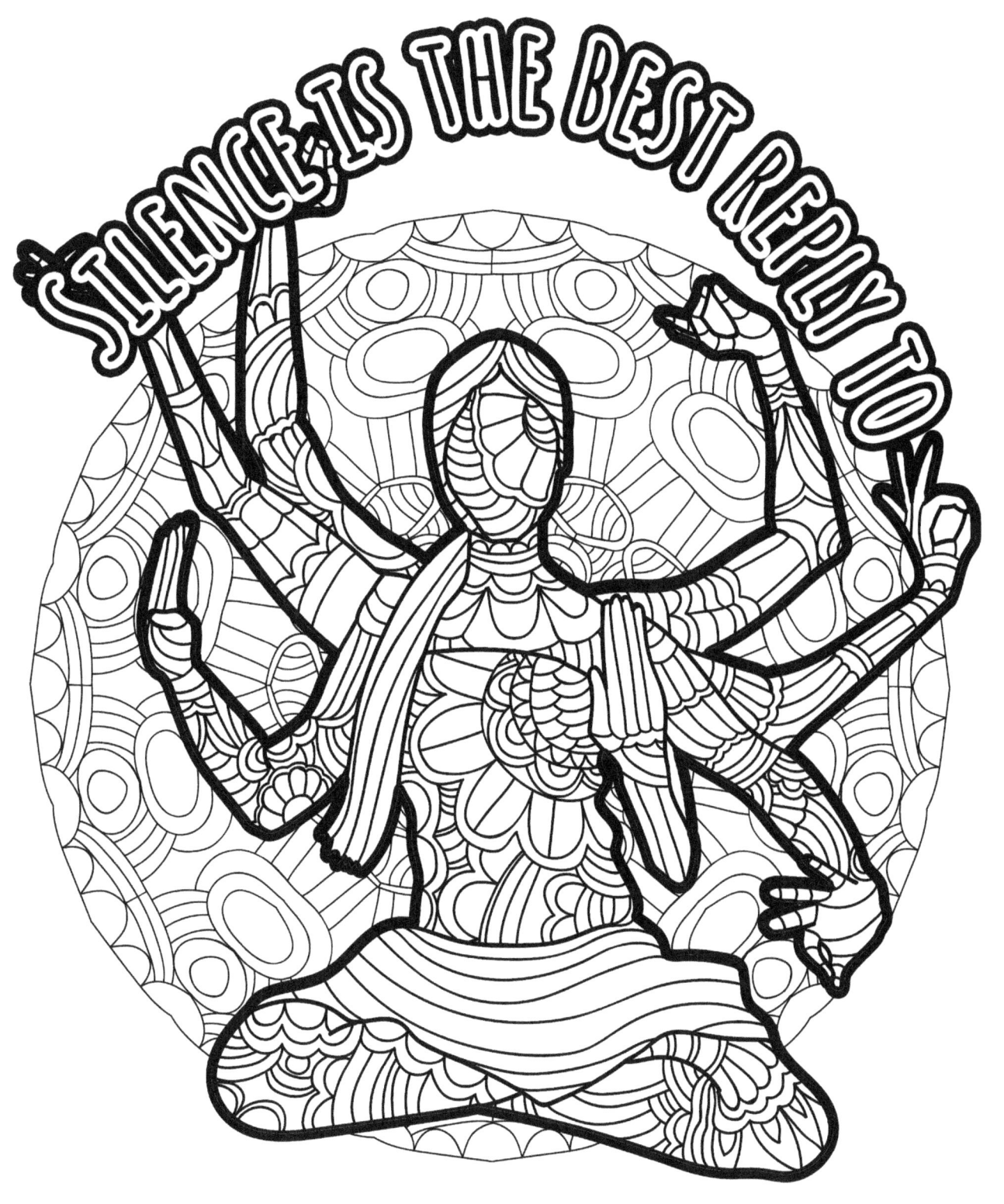

SILENCE IS THE BEST REPLY TO

A FUCKING FOOL

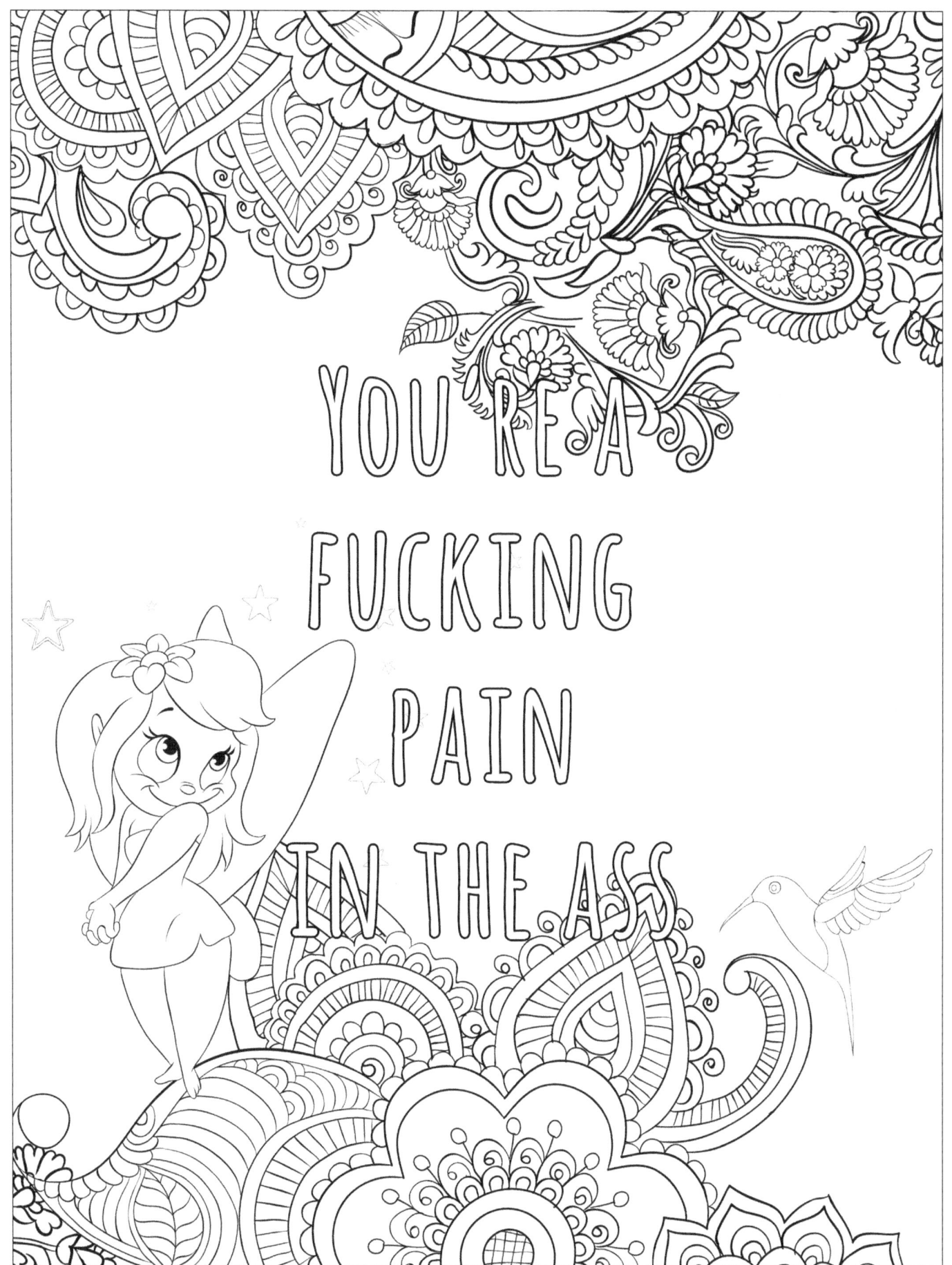

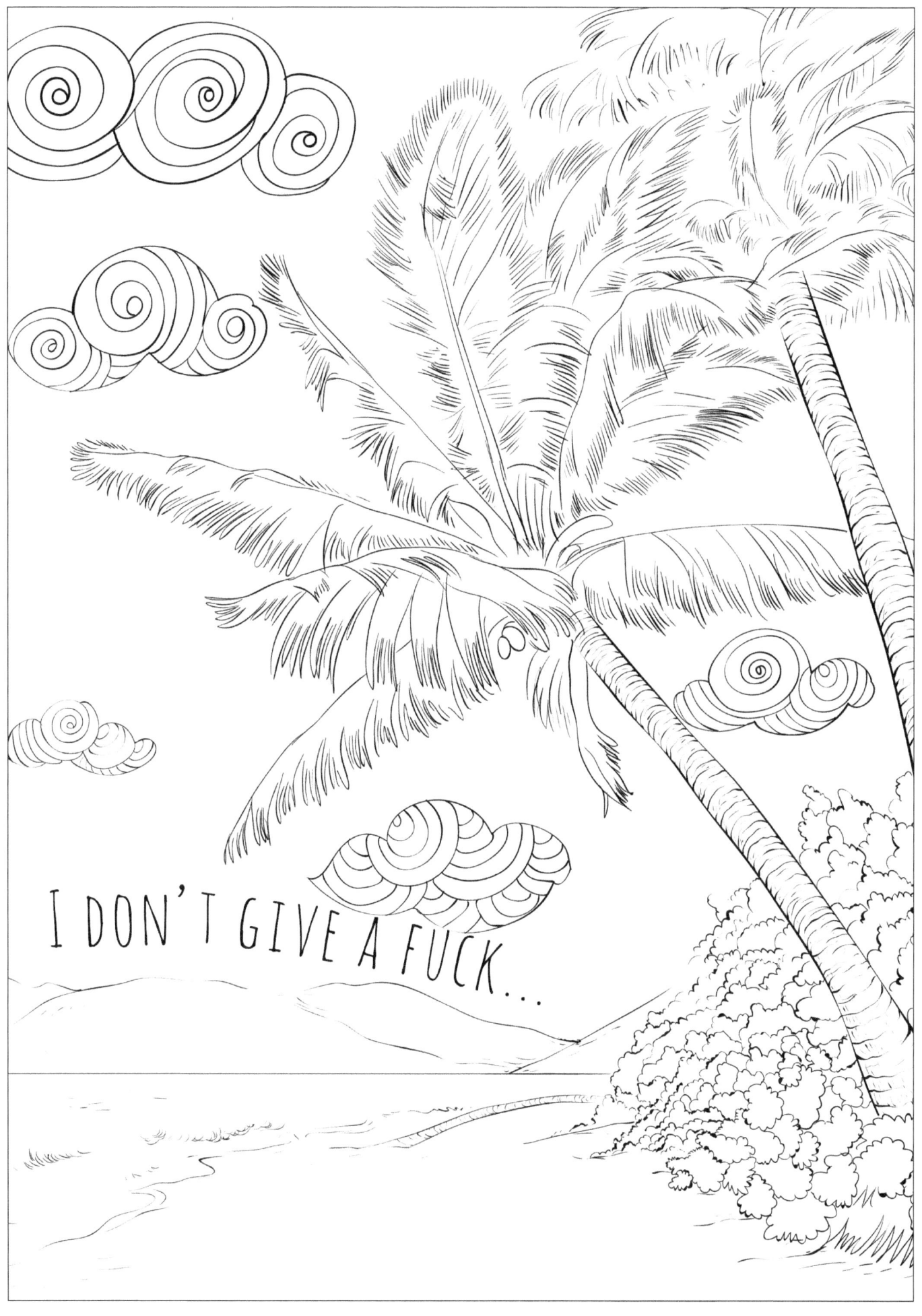

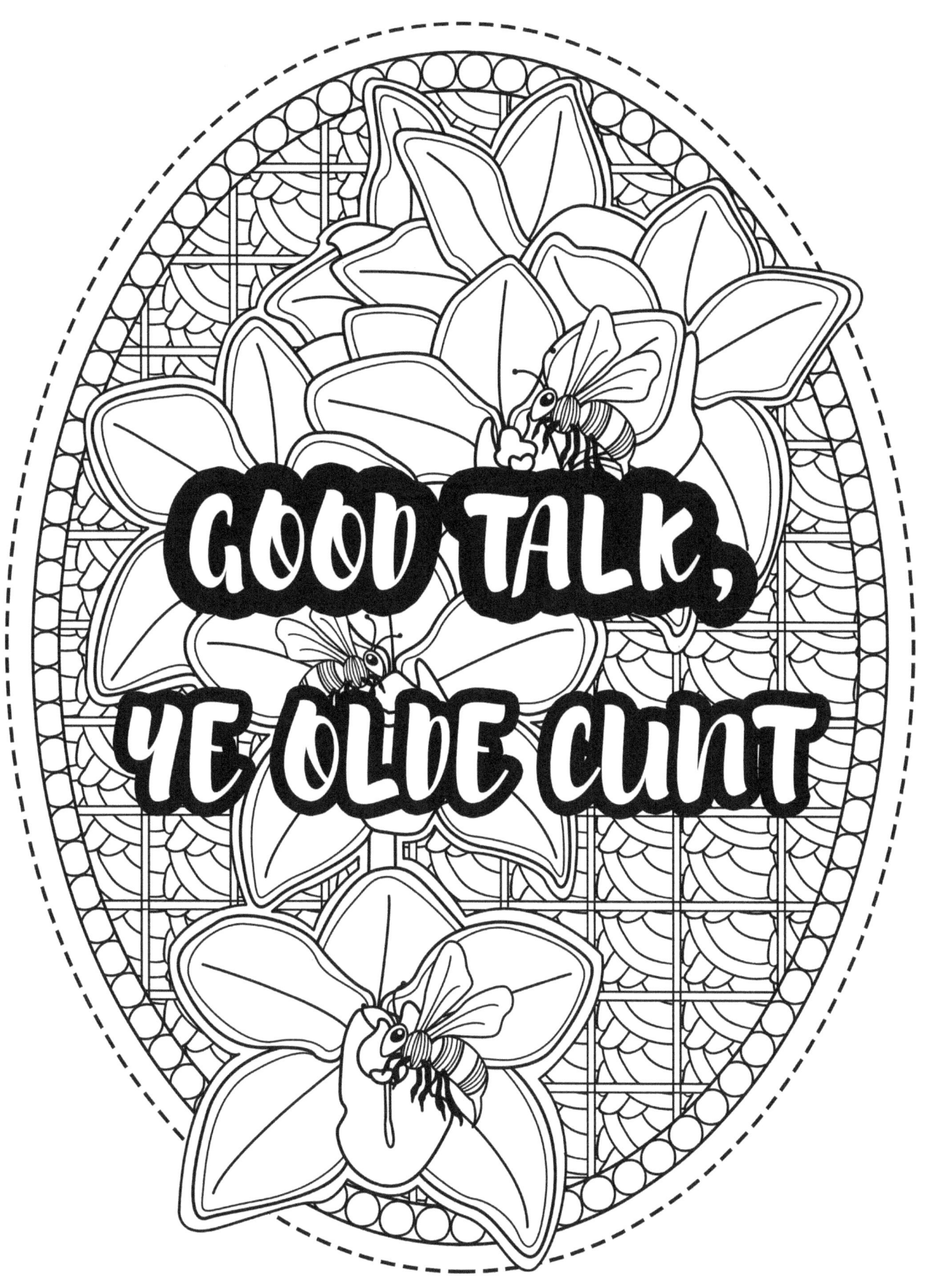

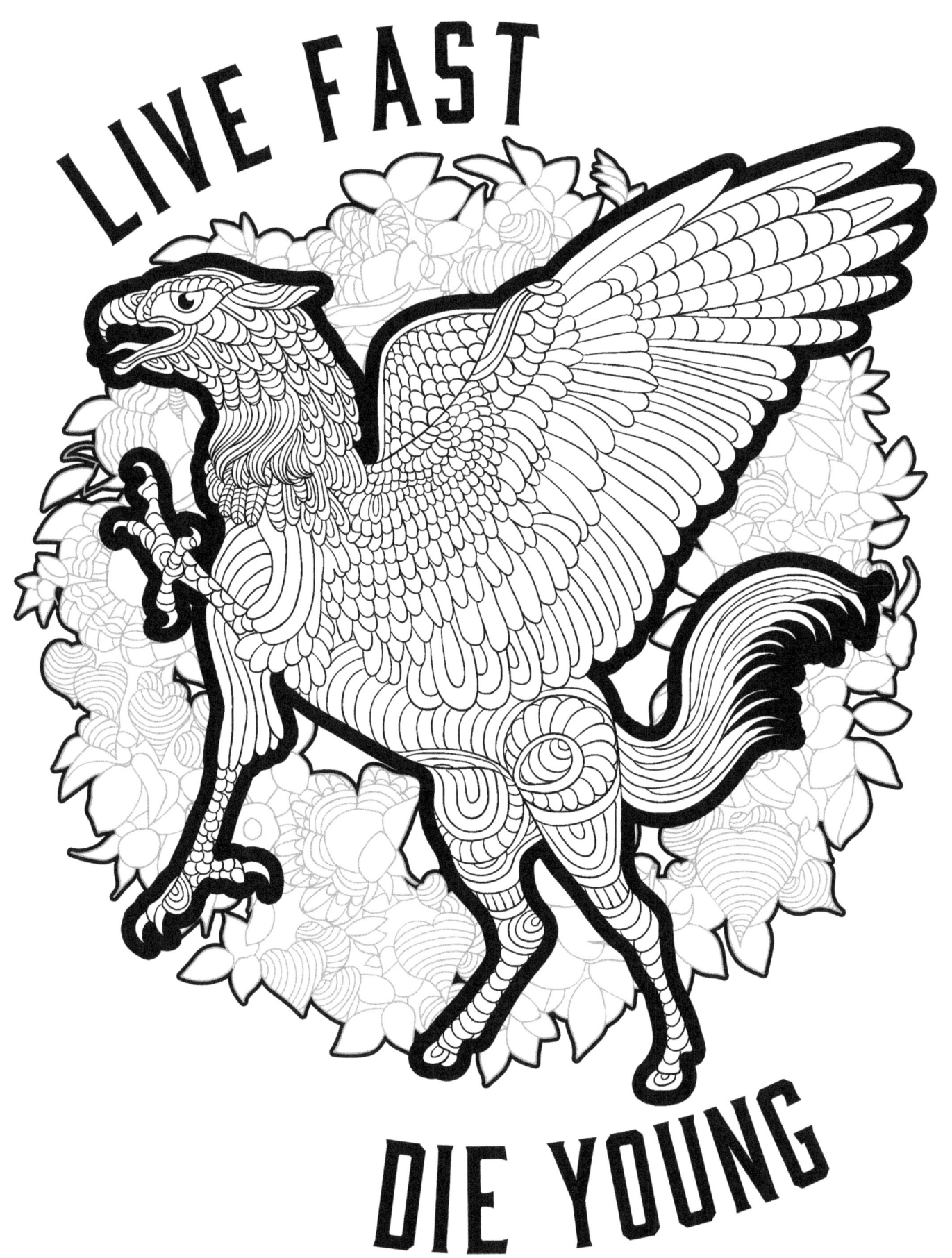

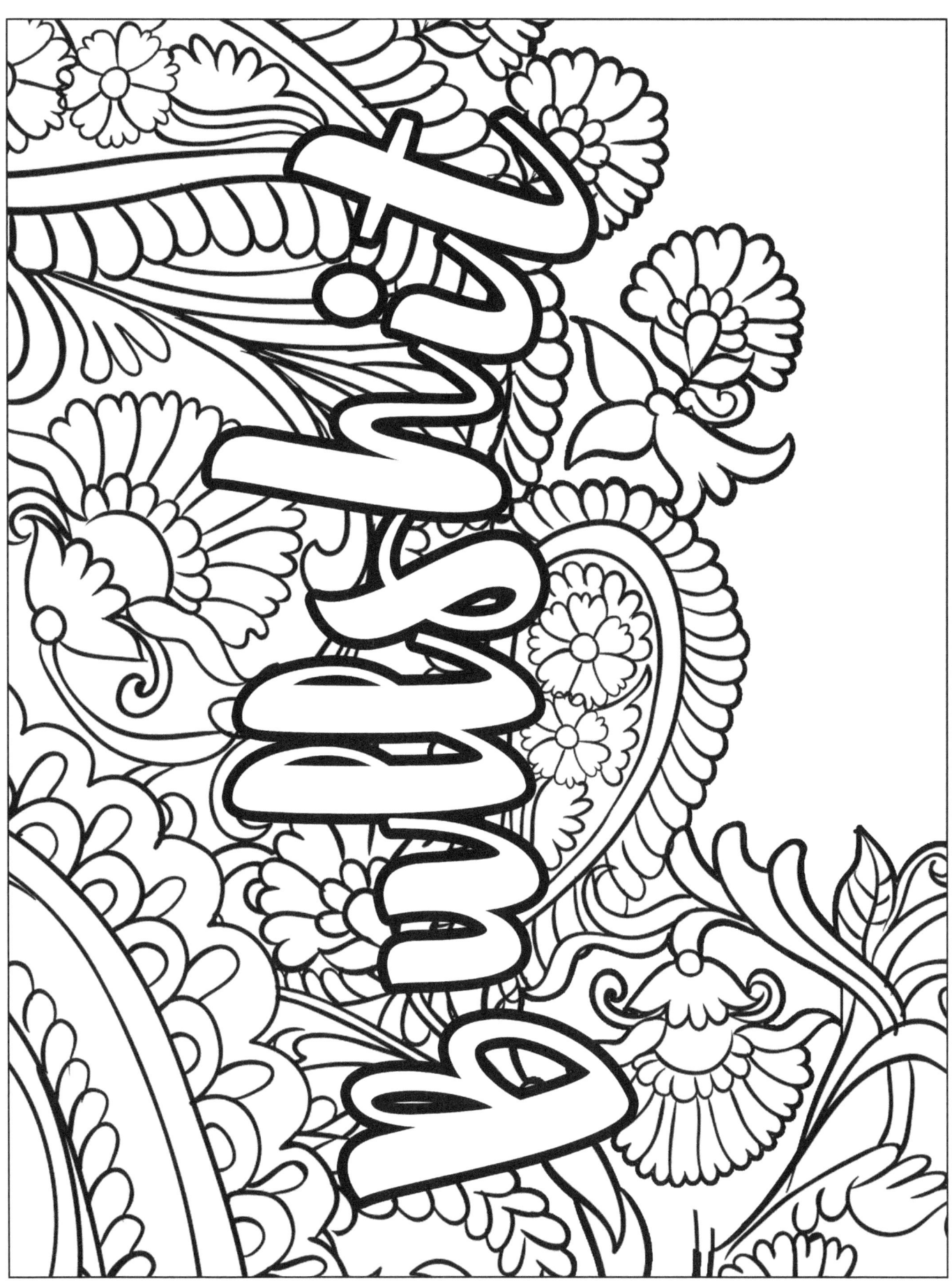

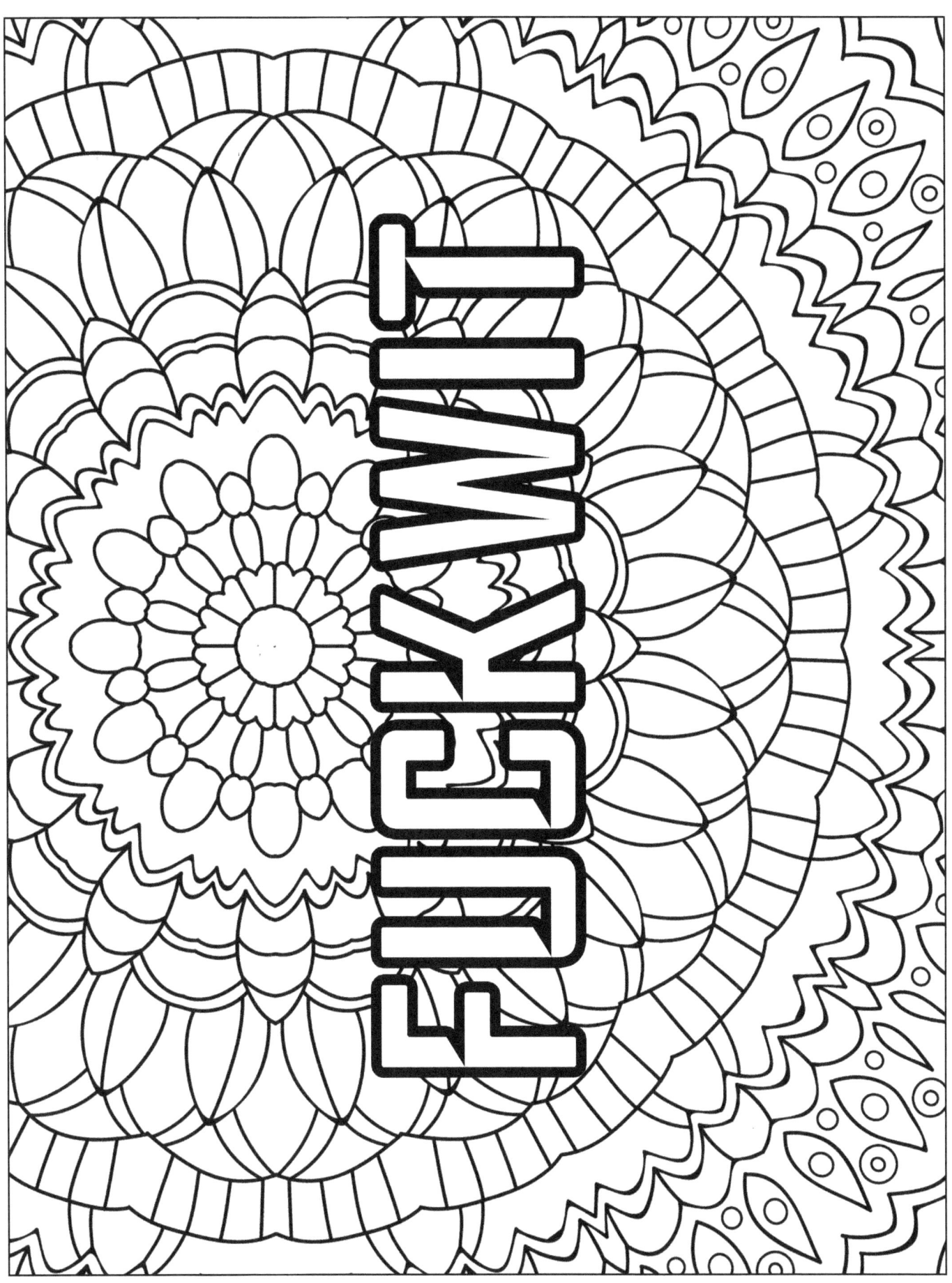

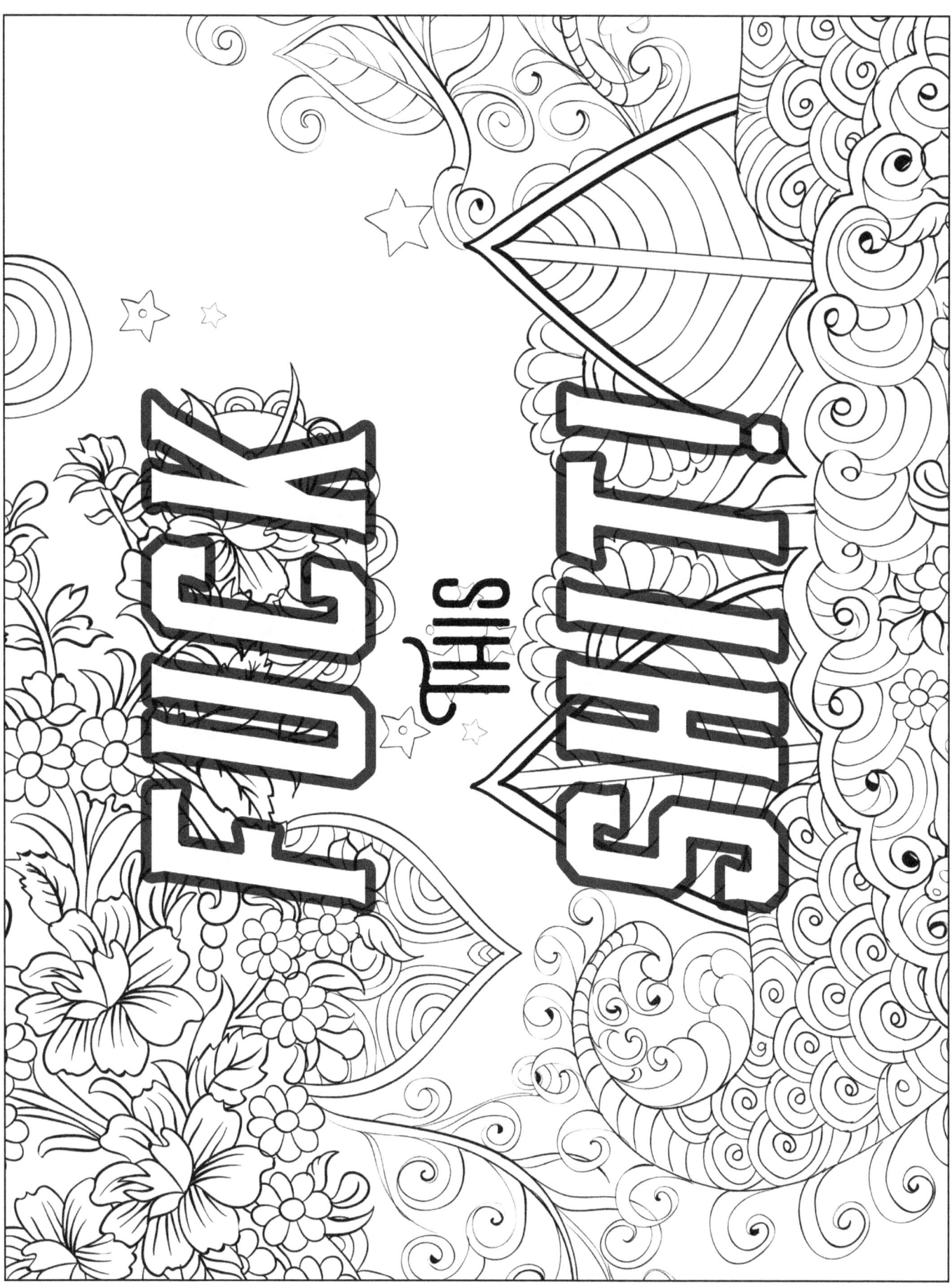

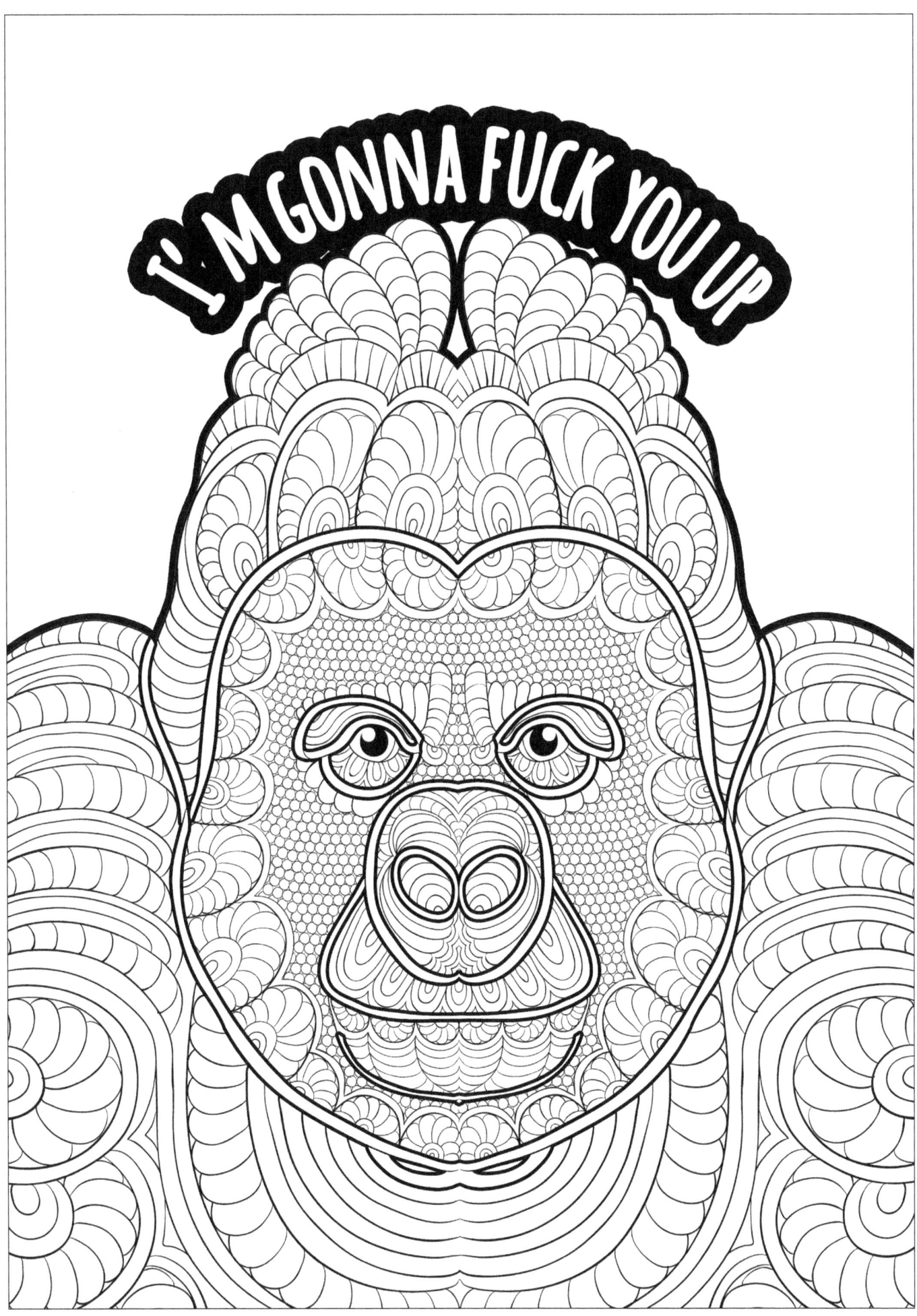

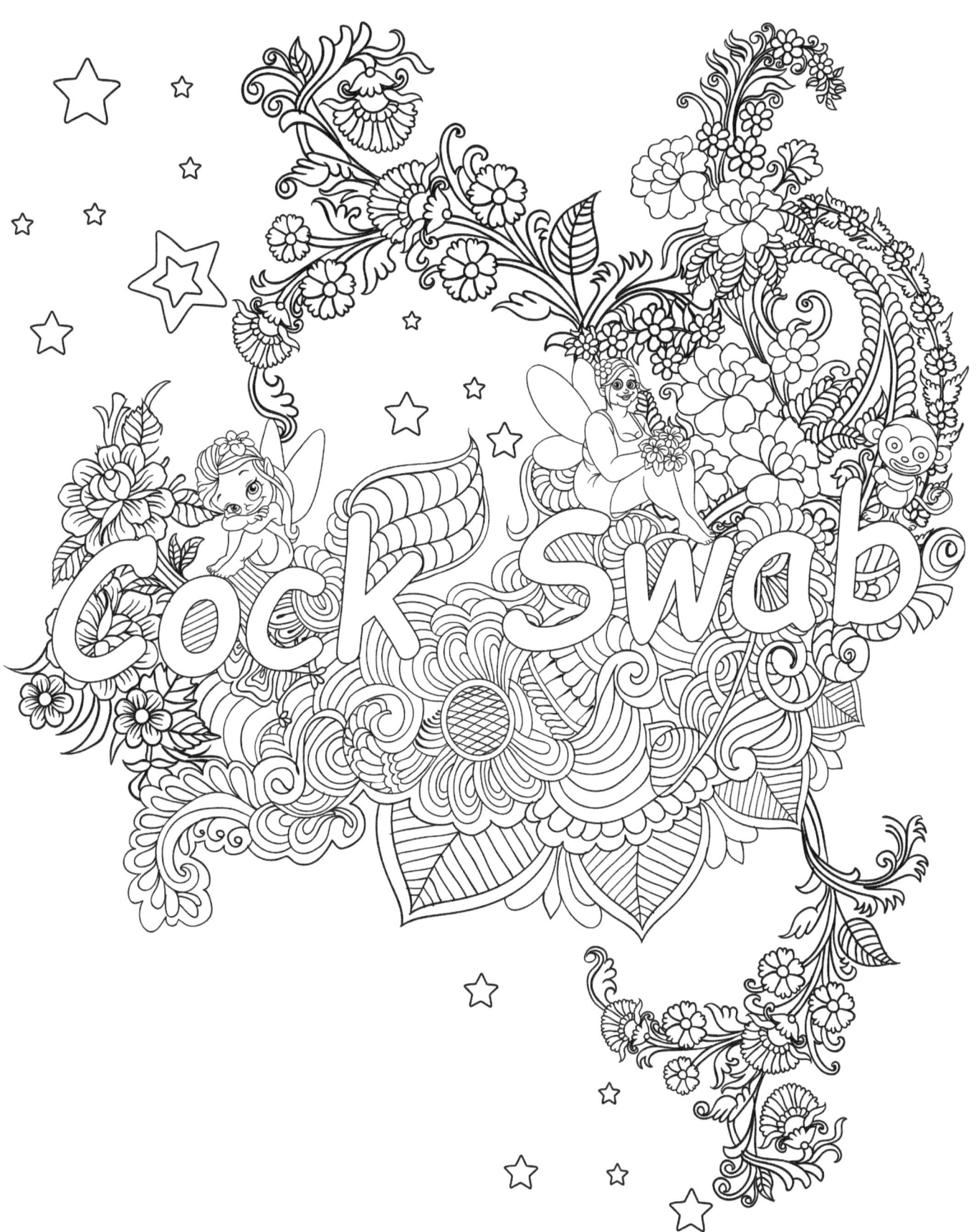

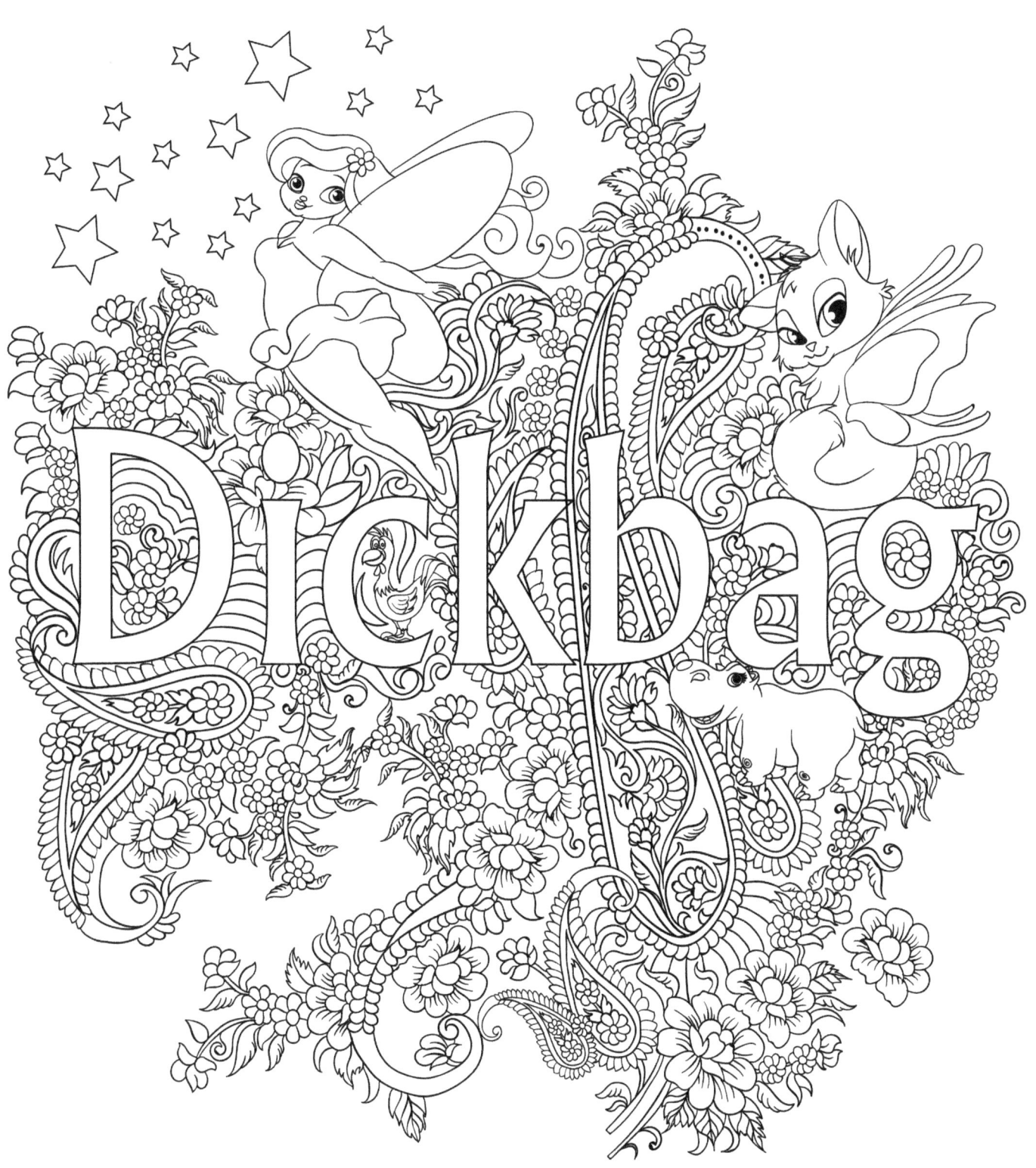

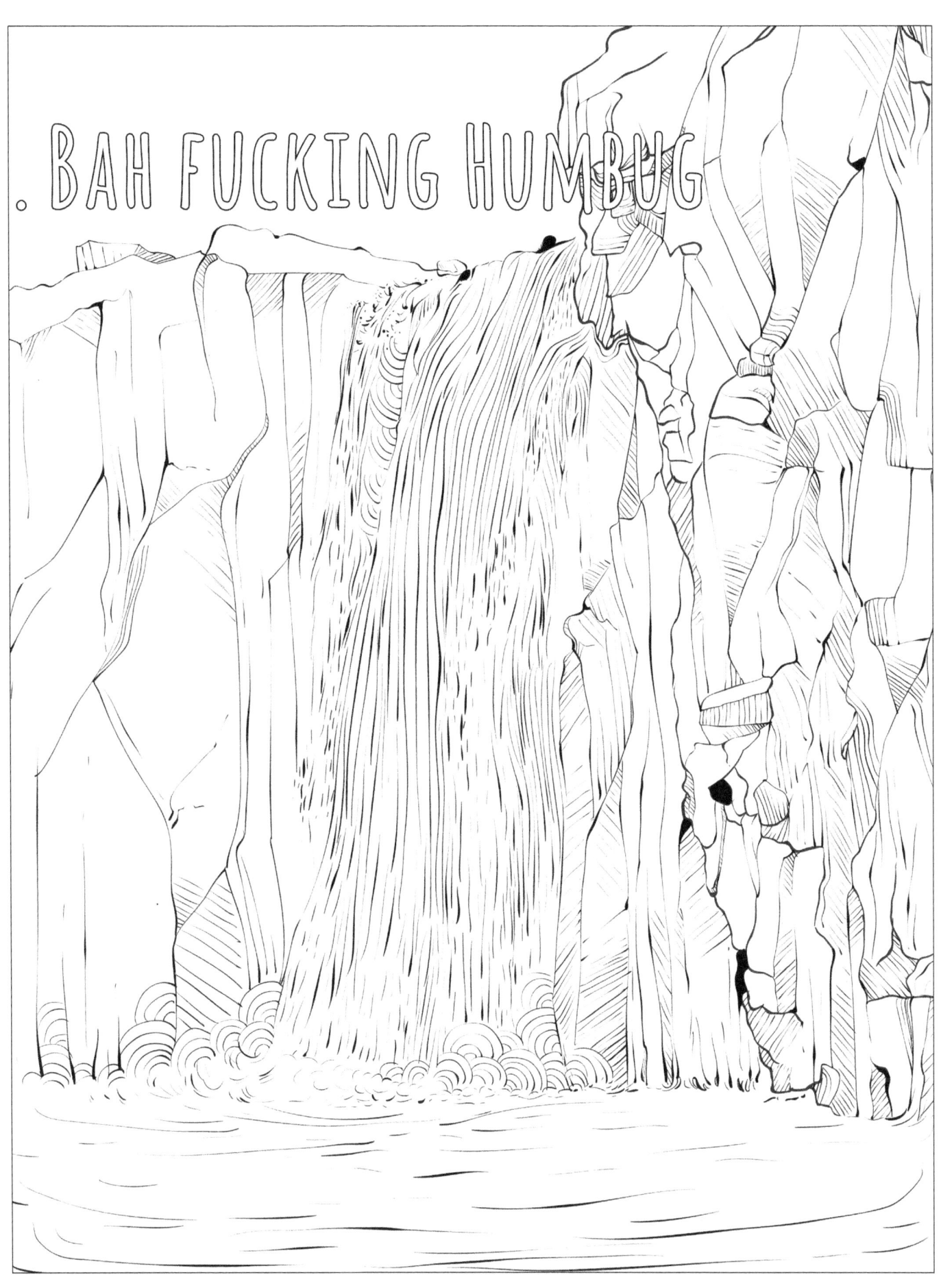

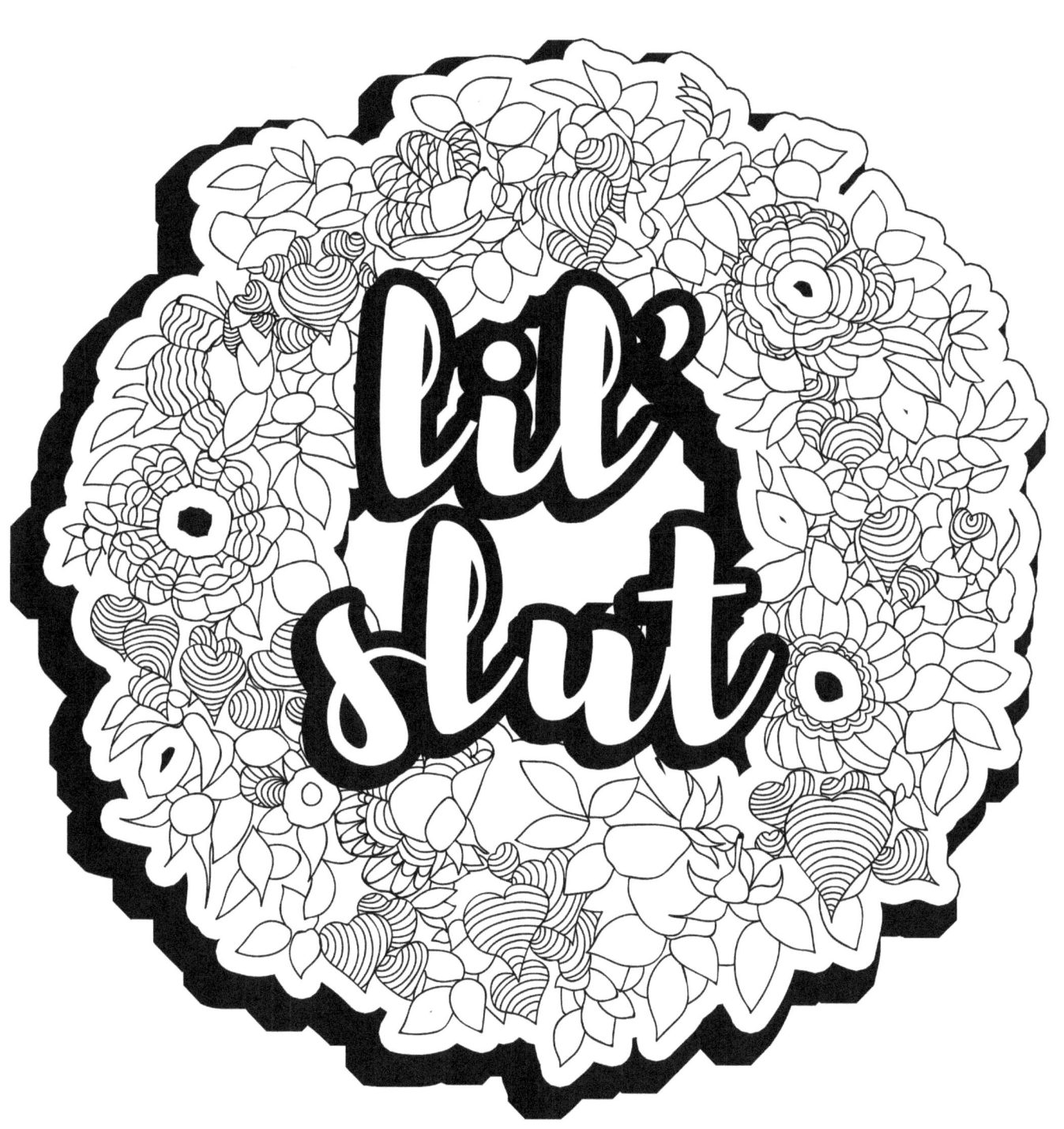

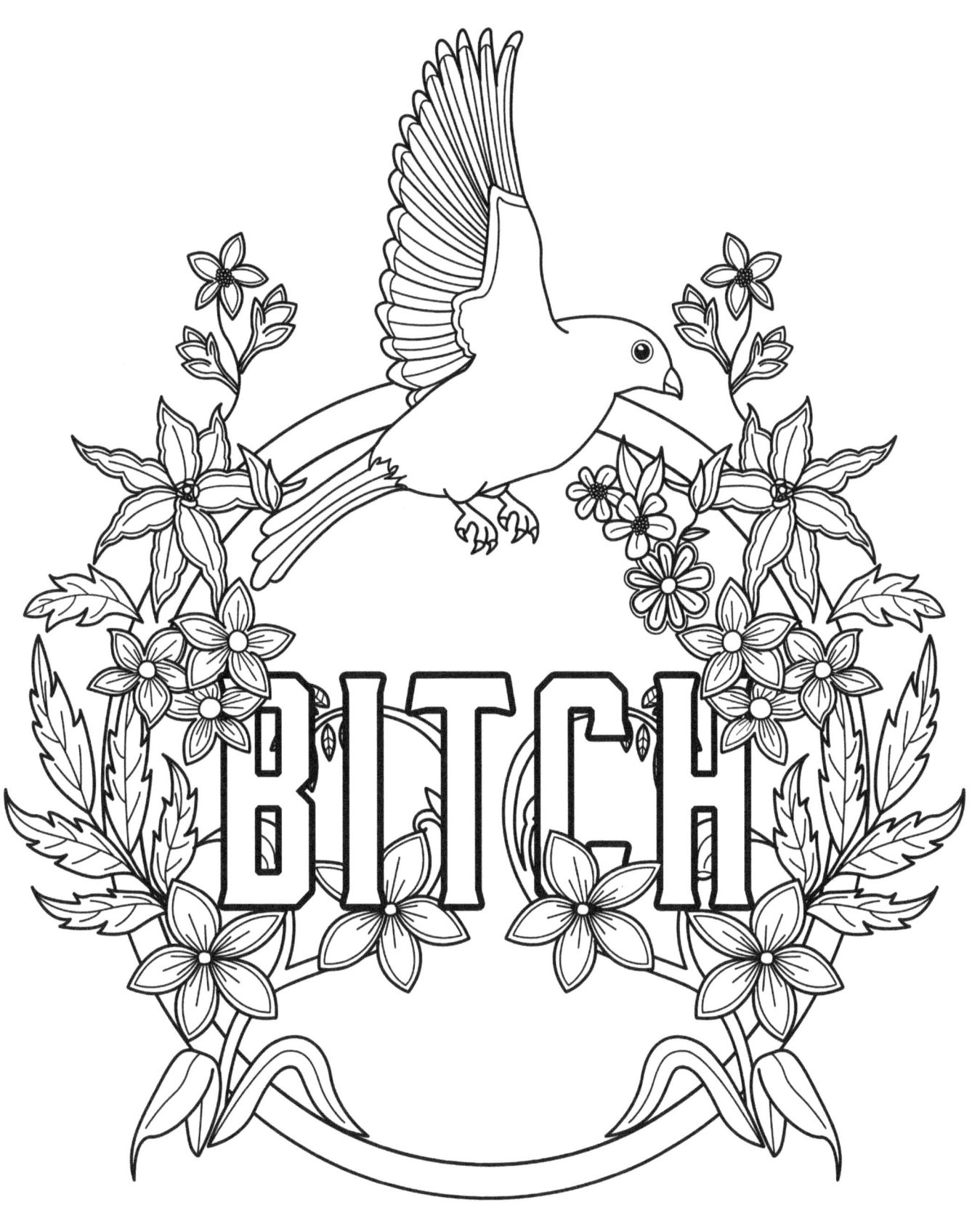

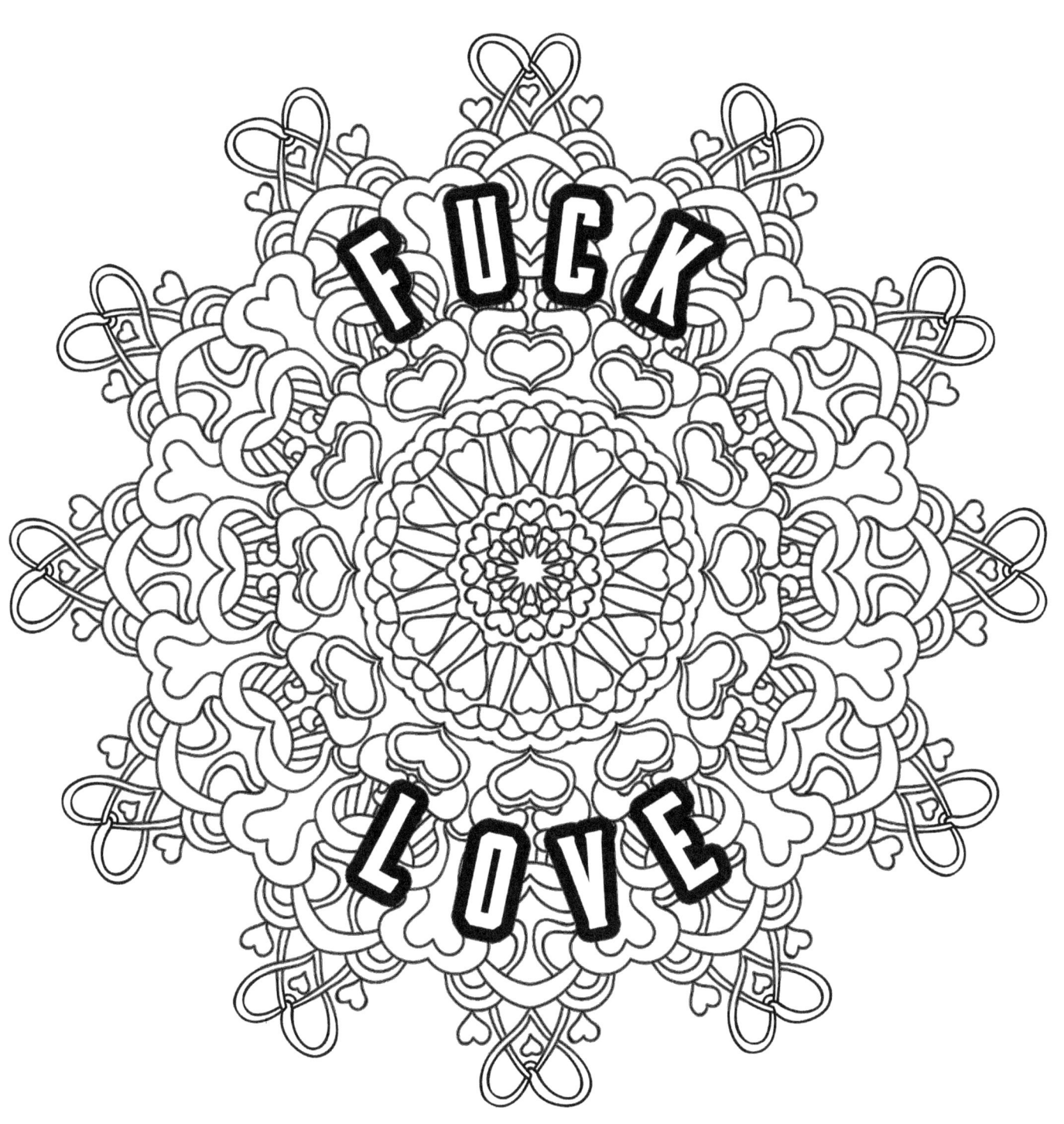

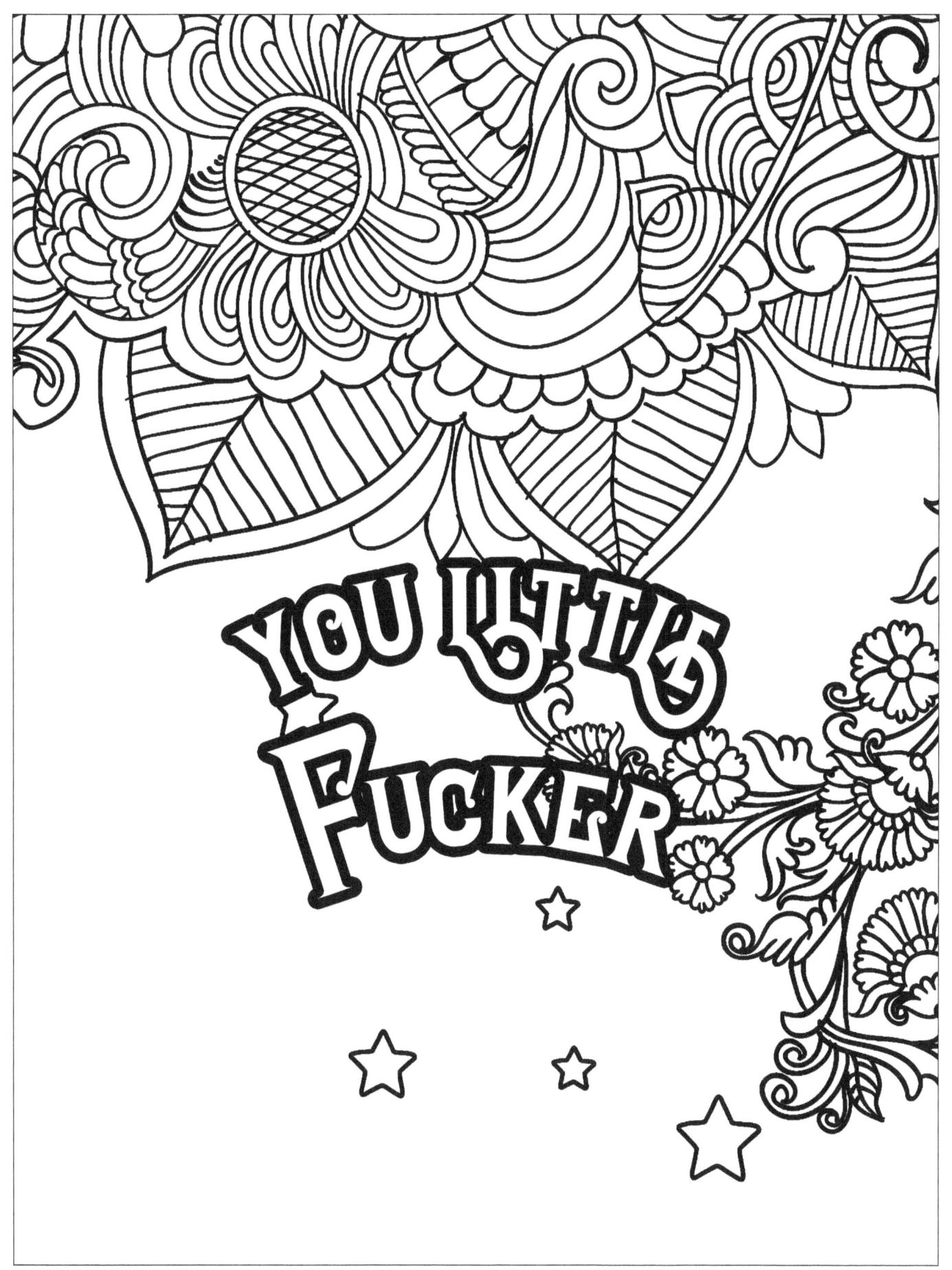

www.ingramcontent.com/pod-product-compliance
Lightning Source LLC
Chambersburg PA
CBHW080636190526
45169CB00009B/3411